Living with

Technology

How Everyday Technology Is
Quietly Rewiring Our Minds,
Habits, and Human
Connections

Brooks B.Calloway

TABLE OF CONTENT

Introduction

We live in a world where waking up to the sound of an alarm clock has been replaced by a smartphone's buzz, where asking questions no longer involves people, but search engines, and where conversations happen more frequently in message bubbles than in person. The line between human life and machine interaction has blurred so much that most of us can no longer remember how life functioned without the constant presence of screens, sensors, or digital signals. Living with technology is no longer a choice, it's a silent arrangement we've made without realizing it, a contract signed not in ink, but in clicks, taps, and swipes.

The journey into this digital coexistence didn't happen overnight. It started subtly, televisions became commonplace, computers entered workplaces, and mobile phones turned into indispensable tools. The internet slowly crept into homes, then into pockets, and eventually into watches, fridges, cars, and even our own bodies through smart health wearables. What began as tools to enhance life have become extensions of our identities. Technology now shapes how we think, learn, work, fall in love, and even how we raise our children. It has evolved from a companion to a decision-maker, from a servant to a silent partner in our day-to-day routines.

Reflecting on this shift reveals more than just advancements in gadgets, it uncovers a massive transformation in how society functions. The idea that technology was merely a utility has been replaced by the reality that it's now a central pillar of our existence. We don't just use it, we depend on it. And in that dependence, something deeper is occurring. Our behaviors are adapting, our attention spans are narrowing, and our relationships are being reframed. We are not just surrounded by technology; we are being shaped by it in ways that are often invisible until we step back and examine the bigger picture.

This book exists because that reflection is overdue. The pace at which innovation moves is so fast that society barely has time to question its effects. With every app downloaded and every update installed, a small shift takes place. Over time, these shifts accumulate and begin to affect our core experiences. What does it mean to have privacy when your devices know your habits better than your closest friends? What does education look like when students can ask AI to complete assignments? How is parenting evolving when children grow up with tablets as their playmates? And what is the future of employment when machines begin to outperform the very people who once built them?

These aren't just philosophical questions, they're realities unfolding around us every day. The goal of this book is not to resist or reject technology but to understand the relationship we now have with it. Awareness is the first step toward balance. It's time we looked beyond the bright screens and smooth interfaces to understand how deeply this shift has changed us as individuals and as a global community.

By tracing the evolution of digital life and analyzing its subtle but powerful grip on our decisions, emotions, and social systems, this book invites readers to pause and reflect. Not to fear what's coming, but to recognize where we are and where we might be headed if we don't begin living with technology more consciously.

Chapter 1: The Age of Silent Influence

In today's world, technology has infiltrated every corner of our lives, so seamlessly that we barely notice its presence. Modern tech, with all its sophistication and power, has become invisible to us. Its influence is felt in ways so subtle that, often, we don't recognize it as a force actively shaping our decisions, habits, and even emotions. The devices we use every day are no longer just tools; they have become integral parts of our daily existence, quietly guiding and influencing us without us ever fully realizing how much control they hold over our choices.

How Modern Tech Has Become Invisible but Powerful

At first glance, technology seems like a collection of gadgets designed to make life easier. But the true power of technology lies in its ability to blend into the background of our lives, making it almost invisible while simultaneously reshaping the way we think and behave. Consider how many hours we spend on our smartphones or how frequently we interact with smart devices, all without giving it much thought. These technologies have moved beyond being mere tools and have become extensions of ourselves. The apps we use, the notifications that pop up on our screens, and the automated features we rely on all work in the background to anticipate our needs, desires, and preferences.

Smartphones are a prime example of how tech has become part of the fabric of our lives. With just a few taps, we have access to a world of information, entertainment, communication, and services. But what most people don't realize is that, with every swipe, every like, and every purchase, the technology behind the scenes is tracking our behaviors, learning from them, and tailoring our experience to ensure that we stay engaged. It's a constant, invisible feedback loop that shapes our world without us being aware of the forces at play. Over time, this continuous interaction has rewired the way we make decisions, often without us even noticing.

From Smartphones to Smart Homes: The Unseen Shift

The shift from basic gadgets to fully integrated, smart technology has fundamentally altered our relationship with the devices we use. Smartphones were just the beginning. Now, technology surrounds us in almost every aspect of our lives, from smart homes that learn our routines to wearables that track our health. These innovations are designed to make our lives easier, but their reach extends far beyond simple convenience.

Smart homes, for instance, are no longer a futuristic fantasy, they are a reality for millions of people today. With devices like smart thermostats, lights, and security systems, technology has integrated itself into the very structure of our homes. These systems not only react to our commands but anticipate our needs, adjusting the temperature based on our daily schedule or turning off the lights when we leave a room. Over time, these devices learn our habits, often becoming so ingrained in our routines that we stop thinking about how they're shaping the environment around us.

The integration of AI and machine learning in these systems means that every interaction we have with our home devices is used to improve the service they provide. Smart speakers that play music or answer questions don't just respond to commands, they also record data about our preferences, habits, and moods. In this way, technology is no longer something we just use; it's something that learns from us and adapts to us, influencing everything from the ambiance of our homes to the way we interact with our surroundings.

Everyday Decisions Shaped by Algorithms

Perhaps the most significant shift we've seen in recent years is the way algorithms have come to shape our everyday decisions. While most people are aware that algorithms power search engines and social media platforms, few realize how deeply these algorithms influence our daily lives in ways that go far beyond what we consciously choose.

Algorithms are behind much of the content we see online. They dictate what shows up in our social media feeds, what news articles we read, and what products are recommended to us. But their influence doesn't stop there. The same algorithms that suggest what to watch on Netflix or what to buy on Amazon are also determining what we see in our search results, which can shape everything from our opinions to our purchasing habits. This system of recommendation and prediction is so ingrained in our daily routines that we rarely question it, even as it shapes our behaviors.

In fact, algorithms have become so effective at predicting what we want that many of our decisions are now made for us. When we open a social media app, the algorithm decides which posts are most likely to catch our attention. When we search for something on Google, the algorithm determines which results are most relevant to us, based on our past searches and online behavior. And when we shop online, the algorithm suggests products it believes we'll be most likely to purchase, often before we even realize we want them.

This shift has made it easier than ever to navigate the digital world, but it has also made us more passive in our decision-making. We are no longer actively seeking out information or products, we are passively consuming what's been tailored to us. While this can feel convenient, it also raises important questions about the role of technology in our lives. How much control are we truly exercising over our choices? And at what point do we stop being active participants in our own lives and become mere consumers of what's been pre-selected for us?

In the age of silent influence, technology has moved from being a tool to an active participant in the decisions we make every day. Its power lies not in loud, obvious interactions but in the subtle ways it guides our actions and shapes our perceptions. From the devices in our homes to the algorithms behind our social media feeds, technology is quietly rewriting the rules of how we live, work, and connect with each other. The real challenge, moving forward, will be learning how to navigate this world of invisible influence, staying aware of the forces at play, and reclaiming our agency in a tech-driven world.

Chapter 2: The Psychology of Tech Dependency

Technology, by design, has tapped into something deep within the human brain. It's not just the convenience or entertainment it offers; it's how it manipulates our psychological wiring without us realizing it. Every ping, vibration, and notification is more than a simple alert, it's a calculated trigger built to capture attention and keep it. In today's world, it's not just about using technology. It's about how technology is using us, shaping our behaviors and training our minds in ways we never consciously agreed to.

Dopamine, design, and digital addiction

At the core of our interaction with technology lies a neurochemical called dopamine. Often called the "feel-good" hormone, dopamine is released in the brain when we experience something pleasurable or rewarding. Tech designers, particularly those in the app and social media industries, have crafted their products to exploit this exact mechanism. Every like, comment, message, or update delivers a small hit of dopamine, reinforcing our desire to check our devices again and again.

These digital rewards aren't random; they're part of what's known as a variable reward schedule, similar to what keeps gamblers hooked to slot machines. The brain begins to crave the next surprise, the next dopamine hit, without knowing when it will arrive. That's why people can scroll endlessly on social media or open apps repeatedly without thinking. The platforms are engineered to make you feel a sense of urgency and reward, pulling you deeper into habitual use. What appears to be harmless interaction quickly becomes dependency.

It's not just social media, games, news apps, and even productivity tools have gamified their interfaces to maximize engagement. Badges, achievements, sound cues, and colorful visuals are all strategically designed to keep users returning. As a result, the human brain slowly adapts to expect these rewards, conditioning us to seek stimulation from our devices and reducing our tolerance for downtime or boredom. Over time, this pattern lays the groundwork for what experts call digital addiction, an overreliance on technology for emotional satisfaction and psychological comfort.

Attention spans and mental fatigue

One of the most immediate effects of this dependency is the deterioration of our attention span. The more we engage with fast-paced, constantly refreshing content, the harder it becomes to stay focused on slower, more demanding tasks. Research has shown that the average human attention span has decreased significantly in recent years, with many struggling to focus for more than a few minutes without reaching for a device. This shift is subtle, but the consequences are profound.

Mental fatigue sets in when the brain is forced to shift focus frequently, especially when juggling multiple apps, tabs, and notifications. This constant switching taxes the brain's ability to concentrate, creating a loop of distraction and exhaustion. People might feel tired without doing anything physically demanding simply because their cognitive resources are drained by the nonstop digital input. The irony is that while technology promises to save us time, it often scatters our focus, leaving us feeling unproductive and overwhelmed.

This fragmented attention also impacts how we consume information. Reading an article from start to finish has become harder for many, as the mind seeks the quick-hit satisfaction of summaries, headlines, and short-form content. It's not just a change in behavior, it's a shift in the way the brain processes and prioritizes information. Deep thinking, critical reflection, and even creativity suffer in a world where the mind is trained to react rather than reflect.

Tech-induced behavior changes we don't notice

While some effects of tech dependency are obvious, like checking your phone every few minutes, others are far more subtle and often go unnoticed. One major shift is in how people interact socially. Conversations are frequently interrupted by screens. Eye contact has diminished. Even moments that used to be reserved for connection, like family meals or outings, are now shared with devices. Without realizing it, tech has redefined the norms of human interaction.

Behavioral patterns are also being reshaped in more personal ways. People may find themselves feeling anxious when their phone isn't within reach, or they may feel phantom vibrations, believing their device buzzed when it didn't. These experiences highlight how deeply ingrained tech has become in our sensory and emotional responses. We've developed behaviors and even physical reflexes around our devices without realizing that the line between man and machine has started to blur.

Beyond anxiety, tech usage affects how we evaluate ourselves and others. Social media platforms, in particular, encourage comparison. Seeing curated images of other people's lives can subtly alter self-esteem, provoke envy, or create a distorted sense of reality. The pressure to document every experience, share every achievement, and seek validation through likes and comments has created a digital mirror in which self-worth is increasingly measured.

Work and productivity have also been affected. Many people now struggle to separate work from personal life due to constant connectivity. Emails, messages, and work updates blur the boundaries of time, making it harder to fully disengage. What used to be personal downtime is now filled with silent pings and digital demands, fostering a culture of burnout and mental exhaustion.

Perhaps most concerning is how early this dependency starts. Children are growing up in a world where screens are their first teachers, entertainers, and companions. This early exposure is rewiring developmental pathways, affecting attention, emotional regulation, and interpersonal skills. The long-term impact of this digital upbringing is still unfolding, but it's clear that the changes are deeply rooted.

Living with technology today means more than using smart devices, it means adapting to a psychological ecosystem crafted to command our time, attention, and emotions. The dependency we face is not accidental; it's the product of intentional design, rewarded behavior, and subtle shifts that often go unchallenged. Understanding this dynamic is the first step in reclaiming balance and awareness in a tech-shaped world.

Chapter 3: Rewiring Human Interaction

Technology has fundamentally altered the way we connect with one another. While it has made communication more accessible and instantaneous than ever before, it has also created a paradox. We are more "connected" than ever, yet more isolated in many ways. The rise of virtual communication has reshaped our social lives, affecting how we form relationships, express emotions, and measure self-worth. But in the process, it has also eroded some of the intimacy and depth that come with face-to-face interactions.

The Rise of Virtual Connection vs Physical Disconnection

The transition from physical to virtual connection has been gradual but inevitable. Gone are the days when a face-to-face conversation was the primary means of communicating with someone. Now, with just a few taps on a screen, we can instantly reach anyone, anywhere in the world. Social media, texting, video calls, and online gaming have revolutionized how we stay in touch, making it easier to maintain relationships despite geographic distances or time zones.

However, this digital convenience comes at a cost. Physical disconnection has become a defining feature of modern relationships. While we may interact with others more frequently, these interactions are often superficial and lacking in the nuances of in-person communication. Body language, tone of voice, and facial expressions, which play a critical role in conveying empathy and understanding, are often lost in virtual spaces. As a result, many people find that while they have hundreds or even thousands of online "friends," they experience a deep sense of loneliness.

Studies have shown that heavy use of social media can contribute to feelings of isolation and loneliness, even as users increase their virtual social circles. The paradox is that while technology has connected us in ways unimaginable just a few decades ago, it has also made it easier for us to feel disconnected from the people who are physically closest to us. People often find themselves scrolling through social media while sitting next to someone, failing to engage in meaningful conversation because their attention is consumed by the digital world.

How Social Media Reshapes Relationships and Self-Worth

Social media has transformed the way we view relationships. It has created new ways to connect with others, but it has also introduced new pressures, expectations, and insecurities. Relationships that once existed privately now unfold in the public eye, with likes, shares, and comments dictating how they are perceived. The constant validation-seeking that occurs on platforms like Instagram, Facebook, and Twitter can distort the way we interact with each other and ourselves.

The act of sharing intimate moments on social media can alter the dynamics of personal relationships. What used to be a private exchange between two people can now be broadcast to an audience of hundreds or thousands. Couples post pictures of themselves on vacation, parents share every milestone of their child's life, and friendships are documented in real-time. While these moments can create a sense of closeness, they also carry the risk of oversharing and eroding the privacy that once defined personal connections.

Perhaps more damaging is the way social media reshapes our sense of self-worth. The pursuit of likes and followers has become a modern-day popularity contest, with many users measuring their value based on their digital presence. This "self-esteem through screens" mentality can create feelings of inadequacy and jealousy when people compare their lives to the highly curated images of others. Social media often presents an unrealistic version of reality, one where everyone seems to be living their best life, leaving those who don't measure up feeling disconnected and inadequate.

The "like" button, for instance, has become a form of social currency, determining who is popular, attractive, or worthy of attention. This constant comparison and the relentless pursuit of external validation can take a toll on mental health, leading to anxiety, depression, and a distorted sense of identity. Social media has shifted the conversation from personal fulfillment and real-world connections to online approval, making it harder for people to find value in themselves without the digital endorsement of others.

Communication Without Emotion: The Emoji Culture

The rise of emojis and GIFs has added another layer to how we communicate in the digital age. While these symbols offer a quick and easy way to express emotions, they also simplify and, in some ways, diminish the depth of human communication. An emoji can convey a smile, a wink, or a heart, but it lacks the complexity and nuance of real-life facial expressions or gestures. Over time, this "shortcut" to emotional expression has altered the way we understand and process feelings.

Emojis, stickers, and other visual cues are now integral parts of how people communicate in texts and on social media. They can soften the tone of a message, express excitement, or show empathy with a quick image. However, these symbols also replace meaningful conversation. People are increasingly turning to emojis to express feelings they might have once communicated with words. The rise of these quick emotional symbols has created a world of communication that is fast and surface-level, making it harder for individuals to have deeper, more thoughtful exchanges.

Furthermore, the overuse of emojis has contributed to a broader cultural shift toward transactional communication. With the pressure to respond quickly, people have learned to convey emotions in brief, shorthand forms. The long, reflective conversations that once defined deep relationships are increasingly being replaced by quick texts and emoji-laden messages. As a result, our emotional expression has become more superficial, reducing the richness of our interactions.

In many ways, the emoji culture reflects the broader trend of reducing human connection to easily consumable content. Just as people now consume news in short headlines or videos in 30-second snippets, they are now conditioned to communicate in similarly bite-sized emotional expressions. While emojis and GIFs make digital interactions more playful, they also contribute to a broader trend of reducing the emotional depth of communication.

Technology has undoubtedly transformed human interaction, but the question remains whether these changes have improved or hindered our ability to connect authentically. While virtual connection has allowed us to stay in touch across vast distances, it has also caused physical and emotional disconnection. Social media has redefined relationships, but often at the cost of real intimacy and meaningful exchanges. And as we increasingly turn to emojis and digital shortcuts to express our feelings, we must ask ourselves whether we are losing something vital in the process, the ability to communicate with genuine emotion and depth.

Chapter 4: The Workplace Reinvented

The workplace is undergoing a seismic shift, one that has been catalyzed by the rapid advancement of technology, particularly artificial intelligence (AI) and automation. What was once a workplace defined by manual labor and human-centric tasks is now evolving into a digital-first environment, where machines and algorithms play an increasingly prominent role in shaping day-to-day operations. The transformation isn't just about new technologies; it's about the way we work, the tools we use, and the very nature of our jobs.

How AI and Automation Are Transforming Jobs

AI and automation have already begun to revolutionize many industries, from manufacturing to healthcare, finance to entertainment. The rise of automation means that tasks once carried out by human workers are now being handled by machines. These machines, powered by AI, can analyze vast amounts of data, make decisions, and even perform creative tasks. In fields like customer service, for example, chatbots and virtual assistants are handling basic inquiries, leaving human employees free to focus on more complex tasks.

While this shift brings undeniable efficiency and productivity gains, it also raises concerns about the future of work. As AI takes on more responsibilities, there is growing uncertainty around job displacement. Entire industries are being restructured, with jobs that once required human expertise being increasingly automated. Roles that once involved repetitive tasks are being replaced by machines that can work faster and more accurately, leaving humans to take on higher-level, strategic functions.

However, the rise of automation also brings new opportunities. As businesses adopt new technologies, new kinds of jobs are emerging that require human oversight and creativity. Roles such as AI trainers, data scientists, and machine learning engineers are now in high demand. While AI may replace certain functions, it also creates the need for skilled workers to manage, develop, and fine-tune these technologies. The key to thriving in this new environment will be adaptability and a willingness to learn new skills that align with the demands of a digital-first economy.

Remote Work, Digital Fatigue, and Hybrid Culture

The COVID-19 pandemic accelerated the trend toward remote work, with millions of workers suddenly finding themselves working from home. This shift wasn't just a temporary solution; it has now become a permanent feature of the workplace for many companies. Remote work has its advantages, including flexibility, reduced commuting time, and better work-life balance. However, it also comes with its own set of challenges, particularly around isolation and digital fatigue.

For many, the boundaries between home life and work life have blurred. The home office has become a central hub for both personal and professional activities, which can create a sense of overwhelm and burnout. The constant pressure to be "always on" checking emails, attending virtual meetings, and managing digital communications, has led to an increase in digital fatigue. Workers are now expected to be more responsive than ever, and the lines between work hours and personal time have become increasingly difficult to maintain.

Digital fatigue is not just a result of excessive screen time; it's also the mental toll of constant multitasking, virtual meetings, and information overload. The shift to remote work has led to more screen interactions, from Zoom calls to Slack chats, with many employees feeling the strain of trying to stay productive and engaged throughout the day. Research shows that digital fatigue is becoming a significant challenge, contributing to decreased productivity, mental health issues, and job dissatisfaction.

Hybrid work models, which combine remote and in-office work, are emerging as a potential solution to this problem. In a hybrid setup, employees can choose when and where they work, balancing the flexibility of remote work with the social and collaborative benefits of in-office environments. The hybrid model aims to provide the best of both worlds, offering workers autonomy and flexibility while maintaining a sense of connection and teamwork.

However, this model isn't without its own set of challenges. Employers and employees alike must find ways to foster collaboration and communication in a mixed environment. The potential for unequal treatment between remote and in-office workers can create divisions within teams, with those in the office gaining more face-time and opportunities for advancement. Successful hybrid work requires careful planning, clear communication, and a commitment to inclusivity.

New Skills in Demand and the Fading Relevance of Others

As technology continues to reshape the workplace, the skills that are in demand are changing. The rise of AI, automation, and digital tools has led to a greater need for workers with technical expertise, such as coding, data analysis, and cybersecurity. These skills are now considered essential for thriving in a technology-driven world.

At the same time, some traditional skills are fading in relevance. Jobs that involve manual labor or routine tasks are increasingly being automated, leaving workers in those fields with fewer opportunities. Professions that once required expertise in areas like clerical work, data entry, or assembly line production are gradually being replaced by machines, which can perform these tasks more efficiently and accurately.

The demand for soft skills, however, remains as important as ever. Skills like emotional intelligence, problem-solving, and creativity are essential in a world where human interaction and innovation are critical. While AI may be able to perform many tasks, it cannot replicate human empathy, intuition, or creativity. As such, workers will need to develop a blend of technical and soft skills to remain competitive in the modern workforce.

One area of skill development that has gained prominence is digital literacy. As technology continues to evolve, workers must be comfortable using new tools, platforms, and software. Whether it's managing virtual meetings, using project management tools, or understanding AI-driven analytics, digital literacy is now a key competency for success. Education systems are responding by incorporating more tech-focused curricula, but individuals must also take responsibility for staying up-to-date with technological advancements.

The workplace is undergoing a profound transformation, driven by AI, automation, and new work structures. While these changes offer tremendous opportunities for growth and innovation, they also require workers to adapt and develop new skills. Remote work and hybrid cultures are reshaping how we work and interact with colleagues, while the demand for technical expertise and soft skills is becoming more pronounced. In this new world of work, flexibility, continuous learning, and adaptability will be the key to thriving in an increasingly digital landscape.

Chapter 5: Family Life in the Digital Age

Family life, like every other aspect of our society, has been profoundly shaped by the advent of technology. As digital tools and devices have become increasingly woven into the fabric of daily life, the way families communicate, parent, and raise children has transformed. Technology has brought convenience and connection, but it has also created new challenges. The dynamic between generations, the way we parent, and the nature of children's learning have all been deeply affected by the rapid pace of digital innovation.

Parenting in a Tech-Driven World

Parenting today is vastly different from what it was just a few decades ago. One of the most significant challenges modern parents face is how to navigate the digital landscape that their children are immersed in. Technology offers a wealth of educational resources and entertainment, but it also presents concerns about screen time, online safety, and the potential for digital addiction. Parents now find themselves tasked with managing not only their own relationship with technology but also their children's use of it.

The rise of smartphones, tablets, and laptops has made it easier for children to access information and connect with others at an earlier age. These devices have opened up new avenues for learning and creativity, from educational apps to virtual classrooms. For many parents, technology is seen as a tool that can enhance their children's educational experience, helping them to stay ahead in an increasingly digital world. However, the challenge lies in balancing screen time with other aspects of life, such as physical activity, sleep, and face-to-face socialization.

One of the most pressing concerns for parents today is the influence of social media on children and teens. Platforms like Instagram, TikTok, and Snapchat have become integral parts of young people's lives, but they also expose children to new pressures and risks, including cyberbullying, body image issues, and online predators. Parents are forced to navigate how to protect their children online while also allowing them to explore and express themselves in the digital space. Monitoring online behavior, setting boundaries around screen time, and fostering open conversations about the risks of digital engagement have become critical components of modern parenting.

Technology's influence on childhood development and education is both promising and controversial. On one hand, children today have access to a wealth of information and learning opportunities that previous generations could only dream of. From educational apps that teach math and reading skills to interactive digital platforms that facilitate hands-on learning, technology has transformed how children acquire knowledge.

Research has shown that technology can be a powerful tool in early childhood education. Interactive apps and games designed for younger children promote problem-solving, creativity, and literacy in ways that traditional teaching methods may not. For instance, children can now learn basic coding skills or explore new languages through digital games. These tools allow for personalized learning experiences, where children can progress at their own pace and engage with content that interests them.

However, there is also growing concern about the overuse of screens in young children's development. Experts caution that excessive screen time can lead to issues such as poor sleep, reduced attention spans, and difficulty with face-to-face communication. The American Academy of Pediatrics recommends limiting screen time for children under the age of two and being mindful of how much time children spend in front of screens, even in educational contexts. Too much screen exposure can also lead to a lack of physical activity, which has serious health implications for developing children.

In addition, there is evidence that excessive screen time can negatively affect social skills, especially in children who spend a disproportionate amount of time playing video games or using social media. While these activities may provide instant gratification and entertainment, they do not foster the same types of social interactions and emotional intelligence that are gained through in-person play and communication. Therefore, many experts argue for a balanced approach to technology use, one that combines the benefits of digital learning with the need for physical activity, emotional connection, and hands-on experiences.

Technology's Role in Generational Gaps

Perhaps one of the most profound effects of technology on family life is its role in creating and widening generational gaps. Today, different generations have vastly different relationships with technology. Older generations, such as Baby Boomers and Generation X, have witnessed the rise of the internet, mobile phones, and social media, while Millennials and Gen Z have grown up in an entirely digital world.

This disparity in digital fluency can lead to misunderstandings and disconnect between generations. Older family members may struggle to keep up with the rapid pace of technological change, while younger generations may feel frustrated by the lack of tech-savviness in their parents or grandparents. This divide can manifest in various ways, parents might feel alienated by their children's addiction to smartphones, while younger individuals might find it difficult to relate to the more traditional, analog ways of life that older generations hold dear.

Technology has also played a role in how families communicate across generations. While older family members may prefer traditional forms of communication, such as phone calls or face-to-face conversations, younger generations are more likely to use text messages, social media, and video calls. These differences can sometimes lead to frustration, with younger generations perceiving older family members as outdated or out of touch, and older generations lamenting the loss of personal, direct communication.

At the same time, technology has created new opportunities for families to stay connected, especially when physical distance is involved. Video calls, instant messaging, and social media platforms allow families to share moments and stay updated on each other's lives, regardless of location. This digital connectivity can bridge the gap between generations, providing an opportunity for older family members to connect with younger ones in ways that weren't possible in the past.

However, it's also important to recognize that technology has created a paradox: while it enables families to connect across distances, it also fosters a sense of isolation within the home. The rise of individual devices, such as smartphones, tablets, and laptops, means that family members may spend more time immersed in their digital worlds rather than engaging in face-to-face interaction with each other. The challenge, then, is to find a balance, using technology as a tool for connection while also fostering the deep, emotional bonds that are built through physical presence and direct communication.

Family life in the digital age is marked by both opportunity and challenge. Technology has redefined how we parent, how we educate our children, and how we relate to one another across generations. While it provides new tools for learning, connection, and convenience, it also brings new complexities that require careful navigation. As we move forward, finding a healthy balance between the digital and physical aspects of family life will be key to ensuring that technology enhances, rather than detracts from, the relationships that matter most.

Chapter 6: Education Reimagined

The landscape of education has undergone a radical transformation over the past two decades, thanks in large part to technological advancements. What was once confined to traditional classrooms with physical textbooks and face-to-face instruction has evolved into an increasingly digital experience. Today, students around the world can access lessons, assignments, and resources from virtually anywhere, thanks to the rise of online learning platforms, digital classrooms, and artificial intelligence (AI) tutors. These innovations are reshaping the very essence of education, fundamentally altering how knowledge is delivered, absorbed, and applied.

Online Learning, Digital Classrooms, and AI
Tutors

Online learning is no longer a niche offering or an afterthought, it has become a mainstream mode of education for millions of students globally. The COVID-19 pandemic accelerated the shift to digital education, as schools and universities were forced to move their courses online to ensure the continuity of learning. What was initially viewed as a temporary solution has now become an integral part of the education system, with online classes, hybrid learning models, and virtual campuses being increasingly normalized.

Digital classrooms, powered by platforms like Google Classroom, Microsoft Teams, and Zoom, have made learning more accessible and flexible than ever before. Students no longer need to be physically present in a classroom to engage with their teachers or peers. They can access lectures, collaborate on group projects, and receive feedback from instructors all through their digital devices. This shift has opened up new opportunities for students in remote or underserved areas, enabling them to participate in education that might have been previously out of reach.

One of the most promising developments in digital education is the integration of AI tutors and learning assistants. These AI-driven systems can provide personalized support to students, helping them understand complex topics and offering tailored feedback based on their individual needs. AI tutors are available 24/7, meaning that students can receive help whenever they need it, whether it's during late-night study sessions or while working on assignments. Unlike human teachers, AI tutors can adapt their teaching style to suit each student's learning pace, offering a truly customized educational experience.

Furthermore, AI can track a student's progress in real-time, identifying areas where they may be struggling and offering additional resources to help them improve. This kind of personalized, data-driven approach to learning has the potential to revolutionize how students learn and how teachers deliver instruction. By automating repetitive tasks and providing instant feedback, AI allows teachers to focus on more meaningful interactions with students, enhancing the overall educational experience.

The Shift from Memorization to Problem-Solving

Historically, the primary focus of education has been on memorization and rote learning, students were expected to absorb facts and information and recall them when needed. While this approach served its purpose in the past, it has become increasingly outdated in today's fast-paced, information-driven world.

In the digital age, the ability to think critically, solve complex problems, and apply knowledge in practical ways has become far more important than simply memorizing facts.

The shift toward problem-solving in education is largely driven by the rise of technology and the need for students to prepare for a future that demands creativity, adaptability, and critical thinking. In a world where information is readily available at the touch of a button, the ability to process and analyze that information, rather than simply memorize it, is a far more valuable skill. Educational systems are beginning to place greater emphasis on project-based learning, collaborative problem-solving, and interdisciplinary approaches that mirror the challenges students will face in the workforce.

Technology has played a crucial role in facilitating this shift. Digital tools and platforms allow students to engage in hands-on learning experiences that encourage them to think critically and solve real-world problems. For example, students can now use coding platforms, virtual simulations, and data analysis tools to work through complex challenges, gaining practical skills that will be essential in their future careers. These tools also encourage students to collaborate with their peers, fostering teamwork and communication skills that are crucial in today's interconnected world.

In this new model of education, teachers are no longer seen as the sole source of knowledge. Instead, they act as facilitators, guiding students through the learning process and helping them develop the skills needed to navigate an increasingly complex world. This shift represents a profound change in how we view education, moving away from the idea of education as the mere transmission of information and toward the notion of education as the development of critical, independent thinkers.

Are We Creating Thinkers or Tech-Dependent Learners?

While technology has certainly revolutionized education, it has also raised important questions about the long-term effects of relying on digital tools and AI in the classroom. One of the most significant concerns is whether we are creating independent thinkers or tech-dependent learners.

On one hand, technology has the potential to empower students to become more self-directed and capable of finding solutions to complex problems. With access to vast amounts of information and powerful learning tools, students can develop the skills necessary to navigate the modern world. The problem arises, however, when students become too reliant on technology, using it as a crutch rather than a tool for enhancement.

For example, AI tutors can offer personalized support and help students work through difficult concepts, but there is a risk that students may come to rely on these systems too heavily. If they are not encouraged to engage in critical thinking or problem-solving independently, they may struggle to function without the aid of technology. Moreover, the convenience of digital tools can sometimes undermine the development of essential cognitive skills, such as memory retention and the ability to focus without distraction.

Another concern is the potential for digital overload. As students spend more time in front of screens, they may become fatigued or disengaged from the learning process. The constant bombardment of information and notifications can also contribute to a decline in attention spans, making it more difficult for students to focus on deep, sustained learning. In this sense, while technology can be a valuable tool in education, it is important for educators to ensure that it does not become a barrier to the development of critical thinking and independent learning.

Ultimately, the question of whether we are creating thinkers or tech-dependent learners hinges on how technology is used in the classroom. When used appropriately, technology can enhance learning and help students develop the skills needed to thrive in the digital age. However, if students are allowed to rely too heavily on digital tools without developing their own critical thinking abilities, there is a risk that we may be cultivating a generation of learners who are more dependent on technology than capable of independent thought.

The future of education lies in finding the right balance between leveraging technology and fostering critical thinking. It is essential that technology is used as a supplement to, rather than a replacement for, traditional learning methods. By focusing on developing students' problem-solving abilities, creativity, and independent thought, we can ensure that technology enhances education without diminishing the core skills that make us truly human.

Chapter 7: The Rise of Smart Living

The concept of "smart living" has become a dominant trend in modern society, with technological advancements weaving their way into the fabric of our everyday lives. The rise of smart homes, wearables, and lifestyle automation has introduced a new era of convenience, efficiency, and interconnectedness. Today, it is no longer just about living with technology, it's about living smart, with technology seamlessly integrated into every aspect of our home and personal routines. However, with these advancements come significant questions about control, privacy, and the extent to which our personal data shapes not only our lives but also the world around us.

Smart Homes, Wearables, and Lifestyle Automation

Smart homes are now a reality for millions of people around the world. With the integration of Internet of Things (IoT) devices, homes are becoming more than just places to live—they are evolving into sophisticated ecosystems designed to enhance convenience, comfort, and efficiency. From voice-activated assistants like Amazon Alexa and Google Assistant to smart thermostats, security cameras, and refrigerators, these devices allow homeowners to control and monitor their environment with ease.

The ability to adjust lighting, temperature, and even play music with a simple command is just the tip of the iceberg. Smart homes offer unparalleled levels of customization, where everything from the opening of blinds to the starting of a coffee machine can be automated.

This interconnectedness creates a living environment that is responsive to the needs of its inhabitants, adapting to their preferences and even learning their habits over time. For instance, a smart thermostat can adjust the temperature based on your daily routine, saving energy and ensuring comfort without manual intervention.

Wearable technology has become an essential component of the smart living ecosystem, offering insights into our health, fitness, and daily activities. Devices like smartwatches, fitness trackers, and health-monitoring wearables provide real-time data on everything from heart rate and sleep patterns to steps taken and calories burned. These devices allow individuals to take a proactive approach to their health, offering personalized insights and recommendations based on the data they collect.

Lifestyle automation takes smart living to the next level by connecting multiple devices and systems to work in harmony. For example, with a few simple commands, you can have your lights dimmed, the thermostat adjusted, and the music set to your preferred playlist, all before you even step through the door. Automation is also playing a pivotal role in areas like home security, with smart cameras and sensors providing real-time updates and alerts to keep your home safe. The convenience offered by these technologies cannot be overstated, as they create a living environment that is intuitive, responsive, and seamlessly integrated into the daily routines of its inhabitants.

Convenience vs. Control: Who's Really in Charge?

While the rise of smart living offers unmatched convenience, it also raises important questions about control and autonomy. As more devices become interconnected and integrated into our homes and daily routines, there is a growing concern about who truly holds the reins when it comes to decision-making. While the idea of a fully automated home is appealing, it also presents a paradox: with the increasing convenience of automation comes the potential for a loss of control.

When we allow smart devices to manage tasks on our behalf, whether it's adjusting the temperature, controlling lighting, or even deciding what music to play, we are placing a great deal of trust in the technology itself. But how much control are we really giving up? In many cases, these devices are designed to learn our habits and make decisions for us, often without our direct input. This can lead to situations where the technology "knows" us better than we do, anticipating our needs and making choices based on algorithms and data rather than human judgment.

The issue of control becomes even more pronounced when it comes to privacy and security. As smart devices collect data on our daily habits, preferences, and behaviors, questions arise about who owns this data and how it is being used. Are we truly in control of the information being collected by these devices, or are we simply the subjects of an ever-expanding network of surveillance? The more we rely on smart devices to manage our lives, the more we potentially relinquish control over the data they gather, which can be exploited by companies, governments, or even malicious actors.

Moreover, as the number of interconnected devices grows, the risk of system failures or breaches increases. A single malfunctioning device or security vulnerability in the system can cause widespread disruption, leaving homeowners without control over critical functions like heating, security, or communication. This reliance on technology creates a delicate balance between convenience and control, one that must be carefully managed to ensure that technology serves its purpose without eroding our autonomy.

How Data Collected at Home Shapes External Systems

One of the most profound implications of the rise of smart living is the vast amounts of data generated by our everyday activities. Every interaction with a smart device, whether it's adjusting the temperature, using a fitness tracker, or making a purchase online, results in data being collected and stored. This data often referred to as "big data", has the potential to influence not only our immediate environment but also the broader systems that shape our society.

For example, data collected from smart homes can be used to improve the efficiency of energy consumption. Smart thermostats, for instance, gather data on when residents are typically home, what temperatures they prefer, and their daily routines. This data can be used to optimize energy use, reducing waste and lowering utility bills. Additionally, utilities can use this data to better forecast energy demand and manage distribution, leading to a more efficient energy grid.

However, the data collected at home can also extend far beyond the boundaries of the household. As we share more of our personal habits, preferences, and behaviors with connected devices, this data is often transmitted to external systems operated by corporations, governments, and third-party organizations. For example, smart appliances and wearables track our consumption patterns, and that data can be shared with companies to create targeted advertising, personalize products, and even influence purchasing decisions.

This data also feeds into broader societal trends, influencing everything from public health initiatives to urban planning. For example, data gathered from fitness trackers can be used to identify patterns in population health, while information from smart cities, such as traffic flow data and energy usage, can help optimize urban infrastructure. While this data has the potential to improve public systems and services, it also raises concerns about privacy, surveillance, and data ownership.

In many ways, our homes are becoming hubs for the collection of personal data, which then circulates into larger ecosystems that shape the world around us. As smart living continues to evolve, it is essential for individuals, corporations, and governments to address the ethical and legal implications of data collection, ensuring that privacy rights are respected and that the benefits of these technologies are equitably distributed. In this new age of interconnectedness, the data generated within our homes is not just a reflection of our personal lives, it is a resource that has the potential to reshape entire industries and societies.

Chapter 8: Surveillance, Privacy, and the Illusion of Security

The growing presence of surveillance technology in our daily lives has become an undeniable reality. From smart cameras in our homes to the omnipresent presence of monitoring devices in public spaces, surveillance tech has become a normalized and often unquestioned part of modern society. While this technology has made it easier for us to stay connected, informed, and secure, it has also raised profound concerns about privacy, autonomy, and the loss of control over personal information. The more we integrate surveillance technologies into our lives, the more we must confront the trade-offs between convenience and privacy, as well as the question of who truly owns the vast digital footprints we leave behind.

How Surveillance Tech Became Normalized

In the past, the idea of being watched, especially in the comfort of one's own home, was seen as invasive and dystopian. But today, surveillance technology is not only widespread, it is often embraced. We have cameras in our phones, security systems in our homes, and even devices like smart speakers that listen for voice commands. While the primary purpose of these technologies is often framed as providing security and convenience, the subtle shift in how we view surveillance has been striking. What was once a concern, an intrusion into our privacy, has become an accepted part of modern life.

The normalization of surveillance technology has been driven in part by the convenience it offers. Smart home security cameras, for example, give homeowners peace of mind by providing constant monitoring and real-time alerts about potential threats. Similarly, location tracking in smartphones allows us to easily find our way in unfamiliar areas and stay connected with loved ones. These technologies, while often pitched as beneficial, have made it easy for individuals and organizations to accept the idea of being under constant surveillance.

Media portrayals of surveillance and privacy, often framed through the lens of crime prevention, terrorism, or even smart city initiatives, have contributed to this acceptance. People are increasingly comfortable with the idea of surveillance cameras monitoring public spaces, as they are often seen as tools for safety and crime deterrence. Additionally, as technology evolves, many people are now used to the idea that their digital behavior is monitored by companies, from the websites they visit to the products they buy. These actions are often justified under the banner of improving user experience, personalizing ads, or enhancing security.

Yet, while the advantages of surveillance technology are evident in certain contexts, such as reducing crime rates or providing better services, its widespread acceptance also comes with significant risks. In many instances, the sheer volume of data generated by surveillance systems, ranging from facial recognition software to location tracking, has created a pervasive culture of monitoring that is far-reaching and sometimes invisible. People often don't realize how much of their personal information is being collected, stored, and shared.

Trade-offs Between Convenience and Privacy

As surveillance technology becomes more embedded in our daily lives, individuals face a crucial dilemma: the trade-off between convenience and privacy. Many people are willing to trade off their personal information and privacy in exchange for the conveniences provided by tech companies. The ability to track packages, monitor home security, and navigate unfamiliar places using a smartphone's location services is undeniably appealing. But at what cost?

When we accept these conveniences, we often sacrifice our personal privacy in ways we may not fully comprehend. Every time we use a device that tracks our movements or monitors our habits, we contribute to the creation of an extensive digital footprint—an ever-growing collection of data about our lives. Companies, governments, and third-party organizations have access to this data, using it to create profiles, predict behavior, and target advertisements. In some cases, this data is sold or shared without our knowledge, leaving us vulnerable to exploitation.

The privacy trade-off extends beyond the digital realm into the physical world as well. Home surveillance systems, while designed to protect against intruders, often require users to provide extensive amounts of personal data. Some systems offer features like facial recognition, which raises concerns about the collection and storage of biometric data. Additionally, many smart home devices are connected to the internet, making them susceptible to hacking and security breaches. As we invite more technology into our homes, the lines between protection and intrusion blur, and we must consider whether the comfort and convenience these systems provide are worth the potential risks to our privacy.

In the workplace, surveillance technologies have introduced similar trade-offs. Employers may implement monitoring systems to ensure employee productivity or safeguard sensitive information. While these systems can increase efficiency and security, they also pose significant risks to personal privacy. Workers are increasingly subject to digital surveillance, from tracking their computer activity to monitoring their movements through GPS-enabled devices. These practices have prompted debates about the balance between workplace efficiency and personal privacy, particularly when it comes to the ethical implications of such oversight.

Who Owns Our Digital Footprint?

One of the most pressing questions in the age of surveillance and ubiquitous technology is the ownership of our digital footprint. From social media profiles and online purchases to the data gathered by wearable devices, the information we generate is constantly being collected, stored, and analyzed by companies. But who truly owns this data? Is it us, the individuals who generate it, or is it the companies and organizations that collect it?

The issue of data ownership is complex and often unclear. While many users are required to accept terms of service agreements that outline how their data will be used, these agreements are often vague and lengthy, with little explanation of how personal data is stored or shared. In many cases, companies claim ownership over the data generated through their platforms, giving them the right to use, sell, or share it as they see fit. This raises important questions about control and consent, especially when it comes to sensitive information such as health data, location tracking, or personal preferences.

A major concern is the lack of transparency surrounding data collection practices. Users often have limited control over what data is collected, how it is used, and who has access to it. In some cases, personal data is sold to third parties for targeted advertising or marketing purposes, without users being fully aware of the scope of this activity. The increasing commodification of personal data has led to calls for stronger privacy protections and clearer regulations around data ownership, with advocates arguing that individuals should have more control over their digital footprint.

Governments, too, are interested in our digital footprint. While surveillance and monitoring technologies are often justified on the grounds of public safety or national security, the collection and use of personal data by governments raise concerns about civil liberties and privacy rights. In some countries, governments have implemented extensive surveillance programs that track citizens' online activity, communications, and movements. The debate over government surveillance is ongoing, with questions about the balance between security and privacy continuing to be a major issue in the digital age.

As surveillance technology continues to evolve and the amount of personal data collected increases, the issue of digital footprint ownership will become increasingly important. To protect our privacy and autonomy, it is crucial that we demand greater transparency, stronger regulations, and more control over how our data is used. Only then can we ensure that the conveniences provided by surveillance technologies do not come at the expense of our fundamental rights to privacy and personal freedom.

Chapter 9: Health in the Digital Era

The intersection of technology and healthcare has ushered in a digital era where medical assistance is more accessible, data-driven, and personalized than ever before. From wearable health monitors to AI-powered diagnostic tools, the ways people engage with their health have transformed rapidly. These innovations promise to enhance the efficiency and accuracy of care, yet they also raise ethical, psychological, and practical concerns, especially when technology begins to replace the human touch that has long been a cornerstone of healthcare. The challenge in this new reality lies in leveraging these advancements while preserving the trust, empathy, and nuanced care that people expect when facing vulnerable moments in their lives.

Modern health tech has quietly embedded itself into daily routines, with millions of people wearing devices that track their heart rate, sleep quality, oxygen levels, stress responses, and physical activity. These wearables not only collect data but also analyze patterns and alert users to potential concerns before they escalate into serious conditions. By delivering health insights directly to the user, they offer a proactive approach to wellness that contrasts with the traditionally reactive healthcare model.

Simultaneously, telemedicine has expanded the definition of what a doctor's visit can look like. Video consultations, remote monitoring, and app-based check-ins have made medical advice accessible from virtually anywhere. This has been a game-changer for people in remote areas, those with limited mobility, or anyone trying to save time without compromising on care. The efficiency of telemedicine, especially during global events like pandemics, has proven invaluable. Medical professionals can now monitor chronic illnesses remotely, track recovery from surgeries, and even offer mental health support via secure digital platforms.

AI has added another powerful layer to this system. From analyzing imaging scans faster than human radiologists to predicting the likelihood of disease based on lifestyle and genetic data, AI is reshaping diagnostic processes. These systems can process thousands of patient records in seconds, identifying patterns and flagging anomalies that may go unnoticed in traditional workflows. For overburdened health systems, this kind of speed and scale can significantly improve outcomes, especially in resource-limited settings.

The Danger of Self-Diagnosis Through Apps

Yet the rise of digital health also has a darker side, one of false confidence and misinformed choices. The convenience of symptom-checking apps, while helpful in theory, has led to a surge in self-diagnosis. These platforms, driven by algorithms and user-inputted data, may oversimplify or misinterpret symptoms, causing unnecessary panic or, conversely, a dangerous sense of reassurance.

Many individuals now turn to their phones before turning to a doctor, using online tools to determine the cause of a cough, a pain, or a rash. While some platforms offer well-researched suggestions, they can't replace the nuanced understanding of a human doctor who considers a patient's medical history, emotional state, and subtle physical cues. Furthermore, online health forums and social media discussions often serve as unofficial second opinions, creating echo chambers where misinformation spreads easily and anecdotal experiences are mistaken for expert advice.

The overreliance on digital tools for medical interpretation can delay proper treatment or encourage unnecessary interventions. A person interpreting mild symptoms as signs of a severe illness may overmedicate or undergo unnecessary tests. Others might downplay serious symptoms based on reassuring app feedback. In both cases, the gap between digital information and clinical accuracy creates a risk that cannot be ignored.

Balancing Efficiency with Empathy in Healthcare

Technology may enhance speed and scale in the medical world, but it doesn't replace the emotional intelligence and empathy that define compassionate care. An AI chatbot can remind a patient to take their medication or suggest a healthy meal, but it cannot detect hesitation in a patient's voice or respond with warmth to someone's fears about their diagnosis. It is this human element that builds trust and provides the emotional comfort often needed in times of illness.

Healthcare professionals are trained to interpret not just symptoms but context, to recognize when a patient's silence might signal distress, or when a gentle touch can provide reassurance more effectively than words. These moments are what make medical care deeply human. With the increasing digitization of healthcare, there is a growing concern that patients may start to feel like data points in a system rather than individuals with unique stories, emotions, and needs.

Medical ethics, too, are being re-evaluated in this new environment. Can an algorithm truly be held accountable for a misdiagnosis? What happens when an AI system suggests a course of treatment that a doctor disagrees with? As we adopt more technology in medical decision-making, questions of liability, bias in AI models, and consent become even more critical. Patients deserve transparency in how their health data is used and clarity on how decisions are made, whether by humans or machines.

The path forward lies in balance. Wearables and AI tools can empower individuals to take greater control of their health, but they should function as supplements, not substitutes for professional care. Telemedicine should increase access without reducing the depth of the doctor-patient relationship. And while digital systems can streamline processes, they must be designed with empathy, ethics, and human oversight at their core.

As technology continues to redefine health and wellness, the goal should not be to replace human care but to enhance it. By focusing on thoughtful integration, safeguarding privacy, and maintaining compassion at every touchpoint, society can ensure that the digital transformation of healthcare ultimately serves the people who need it most not just efficiently, but also with dignity and heart.

Chapter 10: Entertainment Overload

The digital age has made entertainment more accessible, diverse, and immersive than ever before. From on-demand video streaming to expansive online gaming worlds, people are surrounded by endless content that competes for their attention and time. This constant availability has shifted entertainment from an occasional indulgence to an almost automatic habit woven into everyday life. While this might seem harmless on the surface, the consequences of this shift are far more complex. As entertainment becomes both a comfort and a coping mechanism, it quietly influences emotional health, social dynamics, and even our perception of reality.

Endless Streaming, Gaming Addiction, and the
Need to "Escape"

The rise of digital platforms has made it incredibly easy to dive into entertainment at any moment. A simple tap or click opens a world of movies, shows, podcasts, music, or games, all curated to suit personal preferences. The convenience is undeniably appealing, especially after a long day or during moments of stress. But beneath this ease lies a deeper issue: escapism. People increasingly turn to entertainment not just for enjoyment, but to disconnect from life's challenges, responsibilities, and even emotions.

Gaming, in particular, has become more than a hobby for millions. With hyper-realistic graphics, immersive storylines, and multiplayer connectivity, games now offer alternate realities where players can feel powerful, valued, and in control. However, this digital refuge can turn into a trap. Gaming addiction is a growing concern, with some individuals playing for hours, sometimes days, without breaks, damaging relationships, work performance, and even physical health. The line between entertainment and obsession blurs when virtual achievements begin to matter more than real-life goals.

Streaming platforms contribute to this pattern in their own way. With entire seasons released at once and autoplay features nudging viewers to continue, binge-watching becomes almost effortless. It's no longer unusual for someone to finish an entire series over a weekend, sacrificing sleep, social activities, or productivity. This constant escape into fictional worlds can create emotional numbness and a disconnection from real-life interactions.

How Content Algorithms Feed What We Want (and Don't Need)

Much of this entertainment overload is driven by powerful recommendation algorithms that learn user preferences with astonishing accuracy. These algorithms are designed not to inform or inspire, but to keep people engaged. Every click, pause, rewind, or skip is recorded and analyzed, allowing platforms to present a continuous feed of content that aligns with past behavior. The goal is simple: more screen time equals more profit.

While this personalization can seem helpful, suggesting shows, games, or music tailored to individual tastes, it can also limit exposure to new ideas and perspectives. People become trapped in echo chambers of familiarity, consuming content that reinforces existing beliefs and interests without challenging or expanding them. This narrows intellectual curiosity and reduces the likelihood of discovering diverse forms of entertainment that might foster growth or reflection.

Moreover, these algorithms often push content that triggers strong emotional reactions, drama, suspense, outrage, or excitement, because emotional engagement keeps users watching. The result is a cycle where people are fed a stream of intense, attention-grabbing content that may be entertaining in the moment but ultimately contributes to emotional fatigue and overstimulation.

The Psychology of Binge Behavior

At the heart of entertainment overload lies the human brain's natural response to pleasure and reward. Engaging content activates the brain's dopamine system, delivering a chemical rush similar to that experienced through food, gambling, or other addictive activities. The more people binge, the more their brains crave the same stimulation. Over time, tolerance builds, and it takes longer sessions or more intense content to achieve the same sense of satisfaction.

This cycle is compounded by the structure of modern entertainment. Cliffhangers, achievements, badges, streaks, and interactive choices are all carefully designed to exploit psychological triggers and keep users engaged. The fear of missing out (FOMO) also plays a role, especially in social environments where people discuss the latest episodes, updates, or game releases in real time. Staying up to date becomes a social necessity, not just a personal choice.

Binge behavior, while satisfying in the moment, often leads to feelings of guilt, fatigue, and regret. Many people report feeling empty or emotionally drained after long sessions of streaming or gaming, yet find themselves repeating the pattern. The entertainment that once served as a break from stress becomes a contributor to it, creating a feedback loop that's difficult to escape.

The solution doesn't lie in abandoning digital entertainment altogether but in establishing healthier relationships with it. Recognizing when content consumption crosses from enjoyment into avoidance or addiction is the first step. Setting boundaries, taking regular breaks, and diversifying activities can help restore balance. Just as technology enables endless entertainment, it also offers tools for self-awareness and control, if people choose to use them mindfully.

Living with technology means navigating the paradox of abundance: more access, more choice, but also more pressure and distraction. Entertainment, once a form of creative escape, now demands careful moderation to ensure it enriches life rather than dominates it. By understanding the forces behind binge behavior and the impact of content algorithms, individuals can begin to reclaim control, making entertainment a conscious choice instead of a constant default.

Chapter 11: The Culture of Instant Gratification

In an age where answers arrive in seconds, packages show up in hours, and entertainment streams endlessly, waiting has become a forgotten art. Technology has ushered in an era defined by speed and accessibility, conditioning people to expect immediate results in nearly every aspect of life. This culture of instant gratification, while offering incredible convenience, is quietly reshaping the way humans think, feel, and grow. The desire for everything to happen "now" has created a society that struggles with patience, delayed rewards, and the emotional maturity needed to navigate challenges that don't offer quick fixes.

Speed, Accessibility, and the Death of Patience

The essence of modern technology is efficiency. Search engines provide answers before questions are fully typed. Food delivery apps bring meals within minutes. With just a few taps, people can order anything, from groceries to gadgets, without leaving their homes. This efficiency is no longer viewed as luxury; it's the baseline. Anything slower feels broken or flawed. As a result, patience is no longer a virtue, it's a rare skill.

Children growing up in this digital environment are especially impacted. They learn early that they don't need to wait for anything, be it a cartoon, a game, or an answer to a question. Delayed gratification, once considered essential to emotional development, is no longer being practiced in daily life. This shift has profound implications, as the ability to wait, endure discomfort, or work toward a long-term goal is critical to resilience, discipline, and overall maturity.

Adults are not immune to this erosion of patience either. Long wait times on websites, slow-loading videos, or even short buffering delays often result in frustration or abandonment. Relationships suffer when instant responses are expected in messaging. Even career paths are now viewed through a fast-forward lens, with many desiring rapid promotions, instant recognition, or viral success, skipping the slower journey of experience and mastery.

How Fast-Tech Affects Emotional Growth

The emotional cost of this instant culture is subtle but significant. When people are constantly rewarded for minimal effort, they lose the tolerance for frustration and the skills needed to manage setbacks. Emotional growth, built through challenge, struggle, and time, is compromised when every solution is at their fingertips. The discomfort that once built character is now seen as an unnecessary inconvenience.

Social media amplifies this issue further. The validation loop of likes, comments, and shares creates a dependency on instant feedback. If a post doesn't perform well within minutes, it's often deleted or ignored. Self-worth becomes tied to immediate reactions rather than internal value or long-term achievements. This can lead to anxiety, low self-esteem, and a constant need for external approval, emotional pitfalls that stifle deeper personal development.

Moreover, when digital tools provide shortcuts for everything, from editing photos to solving math problems, young minds may not fully engage in the process. Learning is rushed. Reflection is skipped. Emotional depth takes a back seat to convenience. The slow, often uncomfortable journey of truly understanding something is replaced by quick summaries, tutorials, and hacks.

Long-Term Impact on Ambition, Resilience, and Creativity

The long-term effects of this fast-paced culture touch every area of human potential. Ambition, once rooted in long-term dreams and steady progress, is increasingly shaped by the promise of overnight success. People now look for shortcuts to wealth, fame, and influence, often abandoning traditional paths of learning and effort. When results aren't immediate, interest fades. This mindset diminishes perseverance, a key trait for anyone aiming to build or create something meaningful.

Resilience, too, suffers in a world that minimizes struggle. Setbacks, failures, and criticism are harder to bear because people haven't been conditioned to navigate discomfort. Instead of working through difficulties, many choose to quit, restart, or distract themselves with easier, more instantly rewarding alternatives. The ability to bounce back from failure becomes rarer, and society starts to lose its depth of grit.

Creativity, which thrives in slowness, exploration, and failure, also finds itself under pressure. True innovation often emerges from boredom, long thinking sessions, and trial and error. Yet the digital environment offers constant stimulation, leaving little room for the mind to wander or reflect. When every moment is filled with fast content, the quiet spaces where creativity grows are pushed out. Artists, writers, and thinkers may find themselves struggling not due to a lack of talent, but due to an inability to disconnect long enough to let ideas breathe.

Living with technology means recognizing both its gifts and its trade-offs. While speed and convenience have enriched modern life in many ways, they come with hidden costs. The culture of instant gratification is reshaping human psychology in ways that are difficult to reverse. To live more fully and meaningfully, individuals must learn to pause, endure, and embrace the slow process of growth. It's in these moments of waiting and working that the deepest lessons are learned and the richest lives are built.

Chapter 12: The Digital Divide

As technology continues to evolve and integrate itself into every layer of society, it becomes easy to assume that its reach is universal. But beneath the shiny surface of digital progress lies a growing chasm that separates those with access, knowledge, and resources from those without. The digital divide, often overlooked in conversations about innovation, remains a pressing issue that determines who gets to benefit from the tech-driven future and who gets left behind. While some navigate smart cities and remote jobs with ease, others struggle to find a stable internet connection or understand the basics of using a smartphone.

Inequality in Access and Digital Literacy

At the heart of the digital divide is unequal access. In many parts of the world, reliable internet remains a luxury, not a norm. Even in urban areas, low-income households often can't afford broadband, updated devices, or the subscription-based tools required to participate fully in modern life. Students may attend virtual classes using outdated phones. Families may share a single device for work, school, and healthcare needs. Meanwhile, others enjoy high-speed connections on multiple synced devices across their homes. This disparity doesn't just represent inconvenience, it limits opportunities.

But access alone isn't enough. Digital literacy, the ability to use and understand technology meaningfully, is just as crucial. Having a device doesn't guarantee one knows how to apply it productively. Many people, especially older generations or those with limited education, struggle with basic digital skills, navigating websites, managing privacy settings, or identifying scams. As services from banks to healthcare go digital, those lacking literacy are left out of essential aspects of daily living. This not only isolates them but creates a cycle of disadvantage that deepens over time.

Tech Privilege vs Tech Poverty

The concept of tech privilege goes beyond just owning the latest devices. It includes access to high-quality education, exposure to innovation, and the ability to leverage technology to improve one's life. Someone born into a connected, well-resourced environment learns from an early age how to navigate and benefit from the digital ecosystem. They grow up with tablets in school, learn coding in after-school programs, and apply to college or jobs online without hurdles. Their understanding of technology becomes second nature, an extension of their reality.

In contrast, tech poverty is marked by exclusion. It affects rural communities, marginalized groups, and economically disadvantaged individuals in both developing and developed countries. It shows up in job markets where candidates are filtered out by algorithms because they lack a digital portfolio or LinkedIn profile. It appears in education systems where students fall behind not due to a lack of intelligence but because they don't have access to a computer or Wi-Fi. It manifests in healthcare, where virtual consultations or health-monitoring apps are out of reach for the people who may need them most.

This divide is not just a social issue; it's an economic one. Businesses depend on digitally literate employees. Governments distribute services online. As the world becomes more digitized, the ability to thrive depends increasingly on technological fluency. Those left behind may find themselves cut off from economic mobility, educational opportunities, and even civic participation.

Bridging the Gap in a Connected World

The solution to the digital divide isn't just giving out devices or offering free Wi-Fi. It involves a multilayered approach that includes policy change, educational reform, and community-driven initiatives. Governments can invest in infrastructure, ensuring even the most remote villages are connected. Schools can incorporate digital literacy into early education, treating it as fundamental as reading and math. Non-profits and tech companies can partner to provide training, mentorship, and affordable devices to underrepresented groups.

At a personal level, those with tech privilege have a role to play as well. Sharing knowledge, volunteering for digital literacy programs, or simply being aware of the challenges others face can make a difference. It's not about charity, it's about equity. A truly connected world doesn't just offer fast downloads and smart homes; it offers equal opportunity.

Living with technology shouldn't be a privilege for the few. It should be a shared experience that uplifts everyone. Closing the digital divide isn't just a moral obligation, it's a necessary step toward a more inclusive and balanced future. As innovation accelerates, bridging this gap ensures that progress serves humanity as a whole, not just the fortunate minority.

Chapter 13: When Machines Think for Us

The integration of artificial intelligence into everyday decision-making is no longer a futuristic idea, it's a present reality that quietly guides countless aspects of modern life. From personalized ads to credit approval systems, AI is increasingly making choices on our behalf, often without our awareness. Its influence stretches far beyond smart assistants and chatbots, silently shaping how we interact with the world and how the world responds to us. As we continue to live with technology, we now face a new question: what happens when machines start to think for us?

How AI Decisions Impact Everyday Life

Artificial intelligence operates behind the scenes in more ways than most people realize. It suggests what we should watch, where we should eat, who we might like, and even how we should commute. Search engines tailor results based on our past behavior, news feeds show what algorithms deem relevant, and job platforms filter opportunities through AI models. Even our email inboxes are sorted by systems that guess what matters most. These small nudges seem harmless but cumulatively begin to alter how we view the world, what we choose, and what we ignore.

Beyond convenience, AI is now influencing significant decisions in fields like healthcare, law enforcement, and finance. It assesses loan eligibility, diagnoses illnesses, and flags individuals for criminal investigations. While these systems are trained to be efficient and data-driven, they often operate in black boxes, leaving users unaware of how and why specific conclusions are reached. The illusion of objectivity masks the reality that AI reflects the biases embedded in the data it's trained on. Thus, a seemingly neutral system can still produce unfair or discriminatory outcomes, ones that deeply affect human lives.

Ethical Questions Around AI in Justice, Finance, and More

As AI spreads across sensitive domains, the ethical implications become harder to ignore. In justice systems, predictive algorithms are used to assess the likelihood of reoffending, influencing bail or sentencing decisions. But if the data used to train these models comes from historically biased law enforcement practices, the results can reinforce systemic inequalities. In finance, automated systems decide creditworthiness or insurance premiums based on patterns in behavior and demographics.

These decisions can appear impartial but may penalize individuals based on factors beyond their control.

The absence of transparency is one of the most pressing ethical concerns. When people are denied loans, job interviews, or parole based on AI decisions, they often have no recourse to understand or challenge the process. Who is held accountable when the system makes a mistake? The creators? The users? The machine itself? As technology evolves, the lines of responsibility blur, leaving critical ethical gaps.

Moreover, the use of AI in surveillance, hiring, and education raises questions about consent and privacy. Are individuals truly opting in to be analyzed and judged by machines, or are they simply unaware it's happening? The right to make informed decisions is slowly being eroded by the quiet encroachment of algorithms.

One of the most complex philosophical debates surrounding AI is its challenge to the notion of free will. Predictive technology doesn't just observe our behavior, it tries to anticipate it, often steering us toward predetermined outcomes. When a navigation app reroutes us, or a music platform auto-plays tracks based on our history, our sense of choice feels intact, but it's already been shaped. We may feel like we're making independent decisions, when in fact we're responding to algorithmic suggestions designed to keep us engaged or optimize for efficiency.

This predictive capability becomes even more troubling when applied to human behavior. If systems begin to determine which students are likely to succeed, which citizens may commit crimes, or which employees are worth promoting, they predefine outcomes in a way that stifles potential and reinforces stereotypes. Instead of empowering us to make informed choices, predictive tech can trap us in cycles based on past data, effectively writing our future without our input.

The question then becomes: are we outsourcing too much of our thinking to machines? Technology was meant to assist, not override human judgment. Yet as we grow accustomed to letting algorithms optimize our time, filter our news, and recommend our relationships, we risk losing the ability to question, reflect, and resist.

Living with AI requires more than just enjoying its benefits, it demands that we remain aware of its influence and limitations. We must advocate for systems that are transparent, ethical, and accountable. Because when machines begin to think for us, the line between assistance and control becomes dangerously thin. To preserve our humanity in a tech-shaped world, we must ensure that thinking remains a deeply human act.

Chapter 14: The Future of Human-Tech Symbiosis

As technology seeps deeper into every layer of our lives, the boundaries between human and machine begin to blur. What once seemed like the realm of science fiction, devices controlled by thought, bionic limbs, augmented perception, is now shaping the reality of tomorrow. The era of coexistence is shifting into one of fusion, where humans and technology don't just interact but integrate. The idea of living with technology evolves into something far more intimate: living as part of it.

Are We Merging with Machines?

The notion of merging with machines no longer feels far-fetched. Innovations in neural implants, wearable sensors, and real-time data feedback are moving us toward an era where the human body and technology form a seamless ecosystem. Devices like brain-machine interfaces allow users to control prosthetics, type with their thoughts, and even transmit emotions digitally. With each advancement, the question grows louder: are we enhancing ourselves, or are we slowly becoming machines?

Tech companies and research labs are racing to create direct links between the brain and digital systems. These interfaces promise to overcome physical limitations, restore lost abilities, and amplify cognition. But they also raise questions about autonomy and identity. If a person can access the internet through thought alone, does their brain remain entirely their own? In a world where software updates can influence how we think or feel, the concept of human agency becomes more complex than ever.

Brain-Computer Interfaces and Human Augmentation

Brain-computer interfaces (BCIs) are at the forefront of this transformation. Devices once designed solely for medical rehabilitation are now being developed for mainstream use. Whether it's enhancing memory, boosting learning speed, or even syncing brainwaves between individuals, BCIs aim to elevate human capacity beyond natural evolution. Coupled with advances in genetic engineering, cybernetic limbs, and augmented reality, we are witnessing the rise of human augmentation, a movement that seeks not just to fix what's broken, but to improve what already works.

Such enhancements challenge traditional ideas about human limits. With memory chips that store information like hard drives and exoskeletons that grant superhuman strength, the definition of "normal" begins to shift. As technology becomes a core part of our biology, the lines between enhancement and inequality also begin to surface. Who gets access to these upgrades? Will enhanced humans have advantages over those who remain unmodified? Technology's promise of equality could, paradoxically, deepen social divides.

What It Means to Still Be "Human" in a Tech-Synced World

As we integrate more deeply with machines, the meaning of being human enters uncharted territory. Is it our biological makeup, our consciousness, or our emotions that define us? If we can alter our thoughts, extend our senses, or interact with others through shared neural links, do we remain the same beings we've always been?

The future of human-tech symbiosis forces us to reconsider core aspects of our identity. Empathy, creativity, and moral reasoning, traits once thought uniquely human, are now being mimicked by artificial systems. Yet even as AI becomes more lifelike and implants more common, there remains something deeply personal and irreplaceable about human experience. Our imperfections, emotions, and unpredictable nature may be the very traits that keep us distinct in a world increasingly defined by machines.

Still, the path ahead will likely see a new kind of existence, where humanity is not lost but evolved. A symbiotic relationship where technology doesn't replace our essence but amplifies it, if managed ethically and consciously. We are standing at the threshold of a hybrid reality, and what we choose to embrace or resist will shape not just how we live, but who we become.

In this unfolding future, the challenge lies not in whether we can merge with machines, but whether we can do so without losing the soul of what it means to be human.

Conclusion

Living with technology should never mean living beneath its shadow. While innovations have given us speed, ease, and expanded possibility, they've also come with invisible costs. From rewired habits to strained relationships and mental fatigue, the digital age has quietly reshaped the human experience. But the solution isn't to retreat from technology, it's to rise above its silent influence by mastering our relationship with it.

How to Live with Technology, Not Under It

The first step toward mastering machines is reclaiming awareness. Recognizing how technology subtly shapes behavior, thought patterns, and decision-making allows us to break free from unconscious dependence. Whether it's questioning the push of an algorithm, pausing before reflexively checking a screen, or setting boundaries between work and rest, small acts of mindfulness can shift power back into human hands. Living with technology must be a conscious act, not a passive one.

This awareness also means refusing to let convenience replace intention. It's easy to fall into autopilot mode, letting devices guide schedules, filter information, or distract from discomfort. But by actively choosing when and how to engage, we keep control over the narrative. Instead of tech shaping us, we begin shaping tech to fit lives that reflect our values.

Creating Balance, Awareness, and Healthy Digital Habits

True balance comes from design and discipline. That means structuring life to include both digital connection and genuine disconnection. Daily routines should have screen-free moments, whether during meals, in conversation, or simply in silence. Families can set shared tech boundaries. Individuals can embrace apps that encourage focus rather than distraction. And organizations can foster a culture where well-being matters more than constant availability.

Awareness isn't just about device use, vit's about purpose. Every swipe, click, and scroll should serve something greater than momentary relief. By building habits around learning, creativity, and authentic relationships, technology becomes a tool that enhances life rather than dulling it. We become curators of experience, not just consumers of content.

A Call to Intentional Living in the Tech Age

At its core, this book has aimed to shine a light on the unseen ways technology is shaping the human story. But more importantly, it is a call to action. A reminder that despite all the screens, signals, and software, we remain the authors of our lives. We choose what matters. We decide how deeply we let machines into our minds, homes, and hearts.

The future will only become more digital. But humanity doesn't have to get lost in the process. Through awareness, balance, and intentional living, we can build a world where tech supports human flourishing, not erases it. Mastering the machines is not about domination or rejection; it's about thoughtful harmony. It's about staying human deeply, imperfectly, beautifully human, even as the world evolves around us.

Because in the end, it's not just about how we live with technology. It's about how we live, period.